FILM AND VIDEO

Contents

FILM AND VIDEO

by
Terry Staples

Editor: Deri Warren
Designer: David Jefferis

Piccolo
A Piper Book

Moving Pictures

In 1995, 'the movies' will be 100 years old. December 28th, 1895 was the first date on which an audience parted with money to watch smoothly-moving photographic images being **projected** onto a screen. The show, which took place in Paris, lasted twenty minutes and cost one franc per person.

The effect of this new invention proved to be enormous. By 1910 film had spawned a huge industry, and created its first 'stars'. In the twenties and thirties, hundreds of millions of people all over the world went to the cinema each week. Most of the films produced aimed simply to entertain. Others contained information, propaganda or social protest.

However, after the Second World War, the film industry faced a major threat from television, which was now being transmitted in many countries. During the battle for audiences, film-makers introduced better sound, bigger screens and gimmicks such as 3-D.

Above: During the 1930's and '40's, weekly cinema-going **was a habit for millions of people all over the world.**

Today, American blockbusters like the *Star Wars* films can still pack out the cinemas. However, overall attendance remains low. In the 1980s, people in Britain go to the cinema on average once a year; in Europe between two and three times; in North America six times a year. It seems that if film is to survive beyond its 100th birthday, it will not be in the kind of cinemas we are used to today.

The Rise of Video

Video is a more recent invention than film, but it is still much older than most people think. In fact, the first video disk went on sale in a London store in 1938.

Although video was originally developed for use in TV, the recent invention of a video projection system means that audiences can watch a video production on a large screen. Film is now being challenged on its home ground.

Seeing is Deceiving

When we watch a film in the cinema, or a television programme at home, we expect to see movement on the screen. In fact, the movement all takes place inside the viewer's mind. This is due to what is called 'persistence of vision'. What this means is that our eyes keep an impression of any image we see for about one-thirtieth of a second after the image has been removed. So, if we are shown a series of still images in very rapid succession, each image blends into the following one in what appears to be a smooth, continuous process.

Flicker-book Pictures

A flicker-book illustrates this principle very well. To make one, take a small blank notebook. On the same spot on each page draw a simple stick figure. Slightly change the position of an arm, or a leg, or both, between one page and the next. When you have finished the drawings – the more the better – flick over the pages in rapid succession and the stick figure will appear to be waving or

kicking, or whatever you have drawn.

Both film and video depend upon persistence of vision in order to create the illusion of movement. When a film is being shot, the camera records the action by taking 24 different photographs per second. Later these photographs (normally known as **frames**) are passed through a projector at the same speed, 24 frames per second (fps). In this way, the action is recreated on the screen.

A video image on TV is made up in the same way. Video works at a different rate from film, and this rate is not standard throughout the world. In Europe the image is formed, broken up and reformed 50 times a second. In North America the rate is 60 times a second.

However, this does not mean that video shows more than twice as many frames as film, because each frame is shown twice. Therefore, the number of different frames screened per second is 25 in Europe, and 30 in North America.

9

Spots and Ghosts

The main difference between film and video is that film is produced chemically while video is produced electronically. Film generally results in a clearer, better-quality image, while video is faster and cheaper.

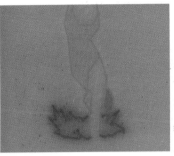

Above: Films occasionally use negatives to create unusual effects, but normally a positive print is needed.

How Film Works

During filming, the film is passed through the camera where it is exposed to light. After this, it has to be sent to a laboratory to be processed. It is this that makes film slower than video, which does not need to be processed. First the film has to be developed, by being soaked in chemicals. This produces a negative, which shows an image of the subject, not in its original colours but in its opposite colours. Thus, blue becomes yellow, green becomes magenta, and red becomes cyan (greenish-blue). This negative could be projected, but it would create a ghostly, other-wordly effect. Normally a positive print is made for projection, so that the colours seen on the screen are the same as those of the original subject.

Layers of Light

All the colours we see on film are made up by mixing red, blue and green light. For example, green light and red light, when they overlap, will produce yellow light.

Modern colour **film-stock** is made up of four parts. In the middle of a strip of film is the 'base', which is simply there to provide a body for the other components to be fixed to. This base is normally made of plastic. Attached to one side of the base are four emulsions – thin layers of light-sensitive chemicals. One of these emulsions is specially made to be sensitive to blue light. Another is green-sensitive, while a third is red-sensitive.

The other layer of emulsion, a yellow one, has a different job to do. Instead of recording light, it blocks it. It stops any blue light that may have got past the blue-sensitive layer from leaking in with the red and green light. Finally, there is a 'backing strip' on the other side of the base. It is there to prevent any light that has passed through all the emulsions from bouncing back and destroying the clearness of the image.

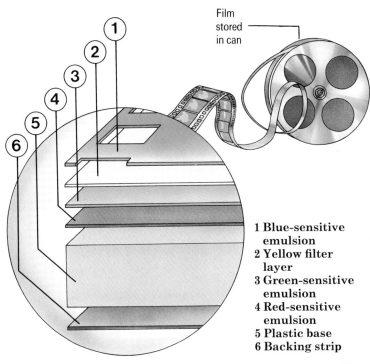

Film stored in can

1 Blue-sensitive emulsion
2 Yellow filter layer
3 Green-sensitive emulsion
4 Red-sensitive emulsion
5 Plastic base
6 Backing strip

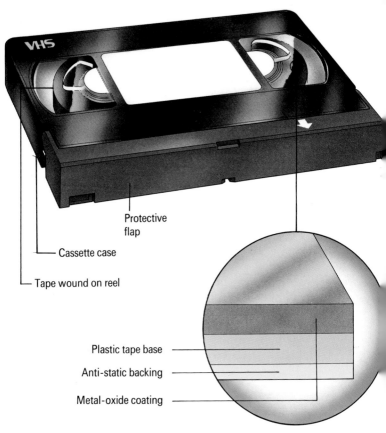

VHS

Protective
flap

Cassette case

Tape wound on reel

Plastic tape base

Anti-static backing

Metal-oxide coating

Dots and Lines

A television image is created in an entirely different way. If you get up very close to a television screen when it is turned off, and stare at a corner of it for a few seconds, you will see that it is made up of thousands of dots. Then turn on the TV, and you will see parallel lines endlessly racing across the screen.

Above: A video cassette, Inset: Cross-section of a piece of video tape.

The dots and lines work in the same way, whether the picture is coming from a live broadcast or from video play-back. They are the result of a system known as 'scanning'.

Scanning is an electronic process which involves a

12

controlled beam of **electrons** sweeping across the inside of the screen. As the electrons hit the light-sensitive dots with which the screen is coated, they cause the dots to glow in particular colours, with varying degrees of brightness. This scanning is done so fast that it is not noticed in normal viewing.

Instant Playback

Video is simply a method of magnetically recording the electronic signals on magnetic tape, so that they can be reproduced later. 'Later', with video, can mean only a few seconds after recording. As soon as the tape has been rewound, it is ready for playback. Furthermore, the sound is automatically recorded alongside the pictures, so the soundtrack is always **synchronized** with the image.

The images may not be as clear as they would be on film, but the immediacy of video is often an overwhelming advantage. For this reason, many rock 'videos' are first shot on film (for quality) and then recorded onto video (for ease of playback).

The tape on which video signals are recorded has, like film, a plastic base. Video-tape, however, has only two added layers. On one side of the base there is a layer of metal-oxide particles which are used to record the video sound and picture (see page 45). On the other side is a layer of carbon which is there to prevent a build-up of static electricity which would ruin the picture.

Below: A TV picture is composed of thousands of little phosphor dots that coat the inside of the screen.

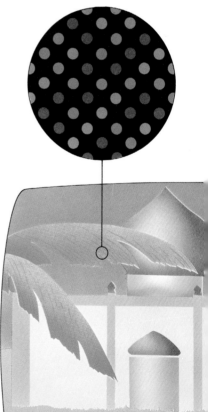

Film and the Cinema

The 1895 film show that marked the birth of the 'movies' combined the new invention of photography with the much older technique of projection. People had been using projection for at least two hundred years. It was based on the principle that if an object is placed in front of a source of bright light, its image will be thrown forward onto a wall or screen.

The use of projection had been very highly developed by the second half of the nineteenth century. Originally, flickering candle light had been used to project the image. This was replaced by **limelight**, which was so intense that it could project an image (usually a picture painted onto a glass slide) from one end of a large public hall to the other. The machine used for this purpose was called a 'magic lantern'.

The images on the screen could be ghostly, comical, spectacular, or a moral lesson teaching right and wrong. Supernatural effects were sometimes obtained by projecting the image of a phantom not onto a screen, but onto smoke. This effect was made all the more impressive when the magic lantern itself was kept out of sight.

Other subjects for slide shows included a man swallowing rats, a clown's performance, a naval battle, making pottery, a fantasy voyage beyond the moon and an illustrated lecture on the evils of alcohol. Some of these shows made extremely skilful use of **dissolves** – that is, making one image fade into another in quick succession.

These dissolves went some way towards creating the illusion of movement. In a show about a famous fire in London, for example, the audience saw the smoke getting thicker and thicker, then the flames leaping higher and higher, and finally the fire dying down as the firemen's hoses played jets of water onto it.

The Challenge of Photography

At first, the slides used in magic lantern shows were hand-painted. Into a circular painting, about 3.5 inches (90 mm) in diameter, artists used to pack a vast amount of brightly-coloured detail. The rigging on a ship, the leaves on a tree, – all could clearly be seen on the screen, even when magnified forty times by a lens in the projector.

By the 1880s, hand-painted slides were being challenged by photographic slides. These were much cheaper to produce.

Left: Watching a magic lantern show.

The Magic Box

Though a camera has sometimes been called a 'magic box', it is of course no more magic than a 'magic' lantern. Both of them are based on a scientific understanding of the nature of light.

A Frenchman named Nicéphore Nièpce was the first person ever to succeed in taking a picture with a camera. In 1826 he used light-sensitive chemicals on a glass plate inside a camera to fix an image of two houses side by side. It took eight hours.

Further developments in France and England soon reduced the necessary **exposure** time to between two and three seconds, in bright sunlight. For sixty years, however, a glass plate, heavy and breakable, remained the only type of base available to photographers. The exposure time, coupled with the weight and fragility of the equipment, meant that early Victorian photography was much better suited to portraits and landscapes than it was at capturing anything in motion.

The most notable exception to this was a photographer named Edweard Muybridge. In 1872 the Governor of California commissioned him to photograph his race horses galloping. To settle a bet, he

wanted to know whether all four legs were off the ground at any one point in time.

After five years, Muybridge managed to solve the problem by placing a long row of cameras side by side on the edge of a race-track. The **shutter** of each camera was connected to a piece of thread stretched across the track. As the horse galloped past, it broke the threads and so released the shutters of each of the cameras, producing glass-plate photographs taken split seconds apart.

Film Speeds Up

In 1888, the Eastman company invented a flexible film base on a roll. Within two years, it became possible to take up to 40 photographs a second.

Sharp-witted showmen soon became interested, sensing the possibility of making money out of the new invention. The public was found to be very willing to put coins into peepshow machines. These worked like a flicker-book, showing photographs at fast enough speeds to create the illusion of movement. These 'movies' lasted less than a minute, and were watched by only one person at a time.

Business was good, but many people saw that it would be even better if film could be projected for a large audience. The race was on.

Below: Muybridge's photographs of galloping horses helped the Governor of California to win a bet.

The First Films

It was this race to combine projection and photography which led up to the 1895 Paris film show. The winners were the Lumière brothers, Louis and Auguste. Working in their father's photographic factory, they devised a machine which could both expose film and project it. This machine, made of mahogany and brass, was called the *Lumière Cinematographe*.

Within two weeks of the Lumières' first public screening, scientists and showmen in other countries had also found a way of combining film and projection. As a result, the 'movies' spread right across Europe and the United States within a year.

The First Documentaries

At first, the only type of films on offer to audiences were what we now call **documentaries**. They were made by setting up the very heavy and immobile camera in a particular place, and filming what was going on. As a

result, a typical Lumière film-show at the end of the century consisted of a collection of short items such as *The Baby's First Lesson in Walking, The Fish Market at Marseilles, A Sack Race between Workers at the Lumière Factory*, and *German Dragoons leaping the Hurdles*. To add to the enjoyment, this last item was shown backwards as well as forwards.

Right: Méliès' *Trip to the Moon* was the first big international success in film history. Many more such trips followed.

Sometimes these films were livened up by having the camera fixed to the top of a train, for example, but it was some years before anyone tried out a totally different approach to film-making.

Méliès – Film Magician

The most successful of the early non-documentary film-makers was Georges Méliès. A magician before becoming a film-maker, Méliès was naturally interested in film's ability to trick an audience. He designed and built the world's first film studio and in 18 years made over 1000 films. Some of them were short trick films, such as *The Man with the Rubber Head*, in which Méliès himself plays an eccentric scientist who blows up his own head like a balloon, till it finally explodes.

He also made some 20-minute science fiction fantasies, based on the novels of Jules Verne. Of these, the most successful was *A Trip to the Moon*.

Bigger and Better

Having found its feet in the last years of the nineteenth century, film set out to conquer the world in the twentieth. Because films were silent, they could be understood everywhere – not just in Europe and America.

During World War One (1914–1918), film production in Europe was interrupted. In America, however, it carried on. By 1920, Hollywood had become the film capital of the world.

Many changes came to film and film-equipment. Audiences had grown tired of short, silent, black-and-white films and wanted something bigger and better for their money. Studios started to make feature-length films (that is, films lasting one hour or more).

The 'Talkies'

It had been possible to record sound for over thirty years before it was successfully joined up with film. Two problems had first to be solved: how to make the actors' speech (the dialogue) satisfactorily match their lip movements, and how to make the sound loud enough for a large auditorium.

Left: *The Black Pirate* was a two-tone Technicolor swashbuckler.

The Western Electric Company produced a solution in 1926. Warner Brothers bought the equipment and made *The Jazz Singer*, in which the star, Al Jolson, had plenty of songs and a few lines of dialogue. Audiences responded with enthusiasm, and producers competed to bring out the first all-talking film. The result of the coming of sound was that audiences in the USA rose from 57 million a week in 1926 to 110 million in 1930.

Glorious Technicolor!

Colour film, like sound, was possible for many years before the Technicolor system became generally accepted. The first Technicolor films used only two colours, red and green. The best-known of these films is *The Black Pirate*, made in 1926 by Douglas Fairbanks. The Technicolor film chemists pressed on, and in six years they had worked out a way of adding blue.

Right: Jolson told audiences 'You ain't heard nothin' yet!'

Scope for Action

Soon after the end of World War Two (1939–45), the novelty of sound and colour began to wear off. More importantly, cinema now had a powerful rival – television.

By the early fifties, weekly cinema admissions in the USA were down to around 50 million. Once again, studio bosses demanded new ideas to bring the audiences back.

The Wide Screen

The most important and successful change made to film in the fifties was the introduction of Cinema-Scope. This was a system based on a special kind of **lens** called an anamorphic lens. In the camera, when a film is being shot, this lens 'sees' a very wide area of action, and squeezes it up onto ordinary 35-mm film. Later, an anamorphic lens, the other way round, is fitted to the projector and stretches out the image so that it regains its proper shape again when it reaches the screen.

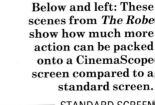

Below and left: These scenes from *The Robe* show how much more action can be packed onto a CinemaScope screen compared to a standard screen.

— STANDARD SCREEN

CINEMASCOPE

Above: This publicity poster gives a rather optimistic impression of 3-D.

CinemaScope was relatively cheap to use because it did not require a new type of film or camera. It did, however, require a much wider screen than the one in standard use.

To fill the wide screen to its best advantage, films were made with plenty of surging action and dazzling spectacle. *The Robe*, a Biblical epic, was the first.

'A Lion in your Lap!'

Another idea developed in the fifties was three-dimensional film, known as 3-D. This attempted to give the screen picture depth, as well as height and width.

To screen a 3-D film, cinemas had to use two separate projectors at the same time, one showing red images, the other showing green. Audiences had to wear special glasses, with one red lens and one green lens. In return, they mostly got things hurled at them, and monsters jumping out at them. After the novelty wore off, 3-D was more or less abandoned, but made a small-scale comeback in the eighties, with *Jaws 3-D*.

23

Cinerama

Many other new film techniques were tried out in the fifties. Cinerama, for example, claimed to bring 'total reality' to the experience of watching a film.

It was based on the fact that our eyes give us a curved view of the world around us – a sweeping arc about 150 degrees wide and 50 degrees high. The Cinerama system set out to achieve the same effect by using three cameras all on the same stand for shooting the film, and three projectors for showing it.

The front rows of the cinema were practically surrounded by the gigantic curved screen, about 30 feet (9 m) high and 90 feet (27 m) round. As well as the normal central projector, a projector on the right side of the auditorium aimed its beam at the left curve and vice versa. The three separate beams were joined up on the screen to make a single image.

At first, Cinerama just made the sort of films that showed off what it could do. For example, audiences of *This is Cinerama* found themselves in the front seat of a roller coaster. Some people felt thoroughly queasy by the end of their 'ride'. In the early sixties a

few Cinerama features were made. After that Cinerama died out, having been found to be too expensive.

Smell-O-Vision and Sensurround

Two other novelties were 'Smell-o-Vision' and, years later, 'Sensurround'.

Smell-o-Vision worked through individual odour outlets installed for each seat in the cinema. The process was controlled automatically by electronic signals on the 'smell-track'.

During the course of a film called *Scent of Mystery*, the audience received controlled

24

whiffs of over thirty different smells appropriate to the on-screen action. Among the smells were boot polish, pipe tobacco, bread being baked, a salty ocean breeze, garlic, carnations, peppermint, coffee, lavender, gun smoke, train smoke and fresh air.

Sensurround tried out the idea of giving the audience something to feel, as well as see and hear. When Los Angeles started to break up in the film *Earthquake*, the audience felt themselves being shaken all over. This effect was achieved by powerful loudspeakers at the back and front of the cinema,

Above: Audiences reacted favourably to Smell-o-Vision and enjoyed being rattled around by Sensurround. Both ideas were short-lived, however.

which gave out a low-pitched rumbling sound.

70-mm Film
One further development worth mentioning is 70-mm film-stock. Twice as wide as standard 35-mm film, it is expensive but it can produce a bigger, sharper image and better quality sound. It is used fairly frequently today.

Cinema of the Future

The IMAX system, invented in Canada in the late sixties, produces the largest film image ever seen. A typical IMAX screen is 45 feet (14 m) high and 62 feet (19 m) wide. The auditorium is very steep, so that every row of seats is about two feet higher than the row in front. This arrangement gives every member of the audience a perfect view of the screen.

To fill this huge area, IMAX uses ordinary film, but in an unusual way. It takes 70-mm film-stock, and runs it through the camera (and later the projector) from left to right rather than from top to bottom. As a result, 70-mm becomes the *height* of the

frame rather than the *width*. This makes an IMAX frame the largest ever used. It is just over 5 square inches (13 square cm) in area, – ten times larger than the frame on 35-mm film.

For the audience, the vastness and clarity of the projected image make it something that they experience rather than just watch. The curved screen stretches either side and up and down, filling the limits of their vision. On top of this, the sound track comes from enormous speakers situated in various places round the theatre. Audience involvement can be total.

So far, the films made in the IMAX system have concentrated on travelling and scenery. One of them, called simply *To Fly*, shows views from balloons, vintage aircraft, helicopters, stunt planes, jets and hang-gliders. It has been playing in IMAX theatres round the world for the last ten years.

The IMAX system is, however, very expensive to install. Also, no-one has yet worked out a way of filming

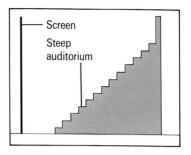

Above: The steep IMAX auditorium raises each row above the one in front, so that everyone can see perfectly.

a full-length entertainment feature with it.

Showscan

Another new process that aims for greater audience involvement is Showscan. So far it has only been seen in America. Showscan uses a screen that is slightly curved, like Cinerama, and letter-box shaped, like CinemaScope. Its film-stock is 70-mm.

What makes Showscan different is its frame rate. It is photographed and projected at 60 frames per second, which is $2\frac{1}{2}$ times faster than the standard rate. The result, its inventor claims, is picture-quality better than anything ever seen before.

Like IMAX, Showscan cinemas have a steep auditorium–but with only 100 seats.

Left: The IMAX screen at Bradford is vast, but the auditorium seats only 320. Showing here is *To Fly*.

Picture Palaces

During the last years of the nineteenth century, film-shows did not last very long. They were usually just one part of a varied bill of entertainment. However, it soon became evident that the public was willing to pay money to be entertained solely by films, and some shops and arcades were converted into cinemas.

On average, there would be about fifteen shows a day. The seats were just ordinary wooden chairs, but the public still kept coming. From around 1905, cinemas began to be designed and built specially. Programmes became longer, and seats became more comfortable.

An Escape into Adventure
The great age of cinema-building began after World War One. In London, some cinemas could seat as many as 3500 people.

The elaborate architecture offered customers an escape from the rather drab post-war world. Some of the cinemas were decorated to look like Chinese pagodas, while others copied Egyptian temples or Spanish villas. They had exotic names such

Left: The luxury of a 1930s cinema in London.

as the *Alhambra* and the *Trocadero*. Inside were marble staircases, glittering chandeliers, mosaic floors, splendidly uniformed staff and plushly padded seats. The best cinemas also had a restaurant and a full-time professional organist who played background music before the programme began.

A New Approach

In the fifties and sixties, as audiences began to fall away, cinemas were forced to close down as fast as they had been put up in the twenties and thirties.

A new way of presenting films has recently worked well in America, and been brought over to Europe. It is called a 'multiplex'. This goes back to the old idea of making the film-show only one among many attractions on offer.

Below: Drive-in cinemas, where audiences watch from their cars, are especially popular in the USA.

Making a Feature of It

The making of a feature film begins when somebody has an idea. If enough people who control the money think that the idea is a good one, then the film might get made. Normally there's a year or two between the birth of the idea and the finished film reaching the cinema screen. However, sometimes this period may be much longer or much shorter.

One of the commonest types of idea is the film-of-the-book. From Méliès to the present day, film-makers have frequently taken books, old and new, as their starting-point. The more famous the book, the more likely it is to be filmed. The Bible has provided stories for countless films, such as *The Ten Commandments*, and Shakespeare's plays have been filmed in many languages. Other famous books brought to the screen include *The Wizard of Oz, Lord of the Rings, The Jungle Book, A Passage to India* and *The Little Prince*.

Stage shows have also been frequently taken as the basis for a film, after running successfully for some years in a theatre. *West Side Story, Grease* and *Oliver* all became films in this way.

Sequels and quickies

If a film is popular with audiences, then producers will normally consider the idea of making a sequel with the same characters and situations. Many recent sequels have just added a number to the original titles – *Rocky 3* for example.

Another type of production idea is the 'quickie', such as *Breakdance* and *BMX Bandits*. Here the intention is to cash in on a fashion quickly, while it lasts. *Breakdance* was planned in January 1984. Shooting began in February. Editing was done in April, and the finished product was being screened all over America in early May. It made so much money at the box-office that the producers instantly produced a sequel called *Breakdance 2*.

Right: The hero is back. *Indiana Jones and the Temple of Doom* successfully repeated the thrill-a-minute formula of *Raiders of the Lost Ark*.

Credit Where It's Due

At the beginning and end of a film, the **credits** are shown. These provide information about who has done what on the making of the film. They show very clearly that film-making is always the result of team-work.

The most important names to appear before the film properly starts, as well as the stars, are the producer and director. The producer has overall control and looks after the money side of film-making, while the director is in charge of the creative side of the film.

Once the subject for the film has been agreed, the

producer has to work out what it is likely to cost. The idea then has to be sold to someone with enough money to invest. Another job is finding the right writer and director for the subject. During the actual filming, the production team also keeps an eye on the day-to-day spending.

One of the director's main jobs is finding suitable actors and then getting their best performance out of them. However, a good performance is wasted unless the film-stock has recorded it satisfactorily, so the director is also concerned with lighting, cameras and other technical aspects. There are normally two or three assistant directors to help – particularly when crowds of extras are involved.

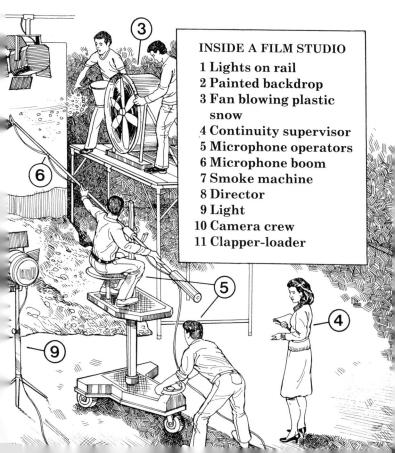

INSIDE A FILM STUDIO

1 Lights on rail
2 Painted backdrop
3 Fan blowing plastic snow
4 Continuity supervisor
5 Microphone operators
6 Microphone boom
7 Smoke machine
8 Director
9 Light
10 Camera crew
11 Clapper-loader

Getting the Look Right

Over ninety years ago, Louis Lumière invented the *Cinematographe*. That term is still important in film-making today. Nowadays, however, a cinematographer is the name given to the person who is responsible for the overall 'look' of the film.

At its simplest, this means that he or she has to make sure that the film passing through the camera is exposed in a way that the audience will be able to clearly see and understand when it reaches the screen. This involves controlling the choice of film-stock, camera-lens, camera-angle and sources of light.

The audience is not always meant to notice the work that goes into cinematography. It often just means that the film is easy to watch. At other times a dramatic use of shadows, or of a **deep-focus** lens, deliberately adds meaning to a shot.

Make-up

Another person concerned with the 'look' is the make-up artist. Over the years, make-up artists have developed a vast range of materials for use in their work. These include wax, plastic, foam, greasepaint, resin, spirit gum, hair, rubber and even special lenses for the eyes.

Every film uses make-up to some extent; some would be absolutely impossible without it. Such films as *Citizen Kane* and *Little Big Man* depended on the make-up artist's ability to age the actors by fifty years or more. Other films, such as *Frankenstein* and *Star Wars*, needed convincing 'monster' make-up. In *Planet of the Apes*, all the main actors except one wore ape make-up throughout the film. For each actor it took five hours each day to apply and remove the ape-mask.

Make-up doesn't only mean sculpting a new face for an actor: it can involve designing and making a complete outfit for a whole body. The gill-man in *The Creature from the Black Lagoon* and the apes in *Greystoke* were created in this way.

Make-up has at last been recognized as a category for Oscar-winning purposes. The first Oscar for make-up went to Rick Baker, for his work on *An American Werewolf in London*, in 1982.

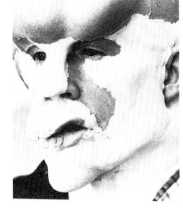

Making up John Hurt to look like *The Elephant Man* was a lengthy and complicated job. The make-up consisted of fifteen separate sections, with each piece overlapping some of the others. It took eight weeks to work it out, and then eight hours each day to put it on. It was extremely uncomfortable to wear. The actor and make-up artist, Chris Tucker, had to start work at four in the morning, so that shooting could begin at mid-day.

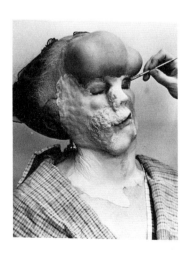

Stunting

Many of the fights and chases that form the high points of certain films would have been impossible to create without stunt doubles. Yet it is only since the seventies that their names have begun to appear in the credits.

Risky Business

In silent films, stars were normally expected to do all their own stunts, however dangerous. Pearl White, who played the heroine in *The Perils of Pauline*, had to climb up the outside of a tall building, be thrown off a cliff, and battle with various savage animals. In one such episode she seriously injured her back.

When that sort of thing happened to a star, it was expensive for the studio. As a result, stars were forbidden to do their own stunts, and doubles took over.

As well as falls and fights, they built up a vast range of 'transfer' stunts. They transferred at high speed from a motorcycle to an airplane, or from a car to a train, or from a horse to a stagecoach.

This last stunt was performed in many films by one of the pioneer stunt doubles, Yakima Canutt. Standing in for the hero, he would ride after a stagecoach going at full speed and gradually haul himself up. Having got to the top, he would fight furiously with the escaping villain. Then he would be knocked off the stagecoach, falling among the galloping hooves. Letting the coach pass over

him, he would grab the rear axle and eventually climb back up to the top to take his opponent by surprise. Yet Canutt's name never appeared in the credits.

The film *Raiders of the Lost Ark* carefully recreated this stunt, using a lorry instead of a stagecoach. However, modern stunt doubles are normally given credit for their work. There was no attempt to pretend that the star, Harrison Ford, had done the dangerous part himself.

Modern technology has produced air bags which cushion a fall without causing a dangerous rebound. Nonetheless, stunting remains a risky job, and doubles sometimes have to say to a director: 'Sorry – that can't be done'.

Below: Mattresses break the fall for this group of Mexican stuntmen.

SCENE 104 TAKE 3 ML
PROD. VID. EXPLAINED
DIRECTOR JEFFERIS
CAMERA P. BAR
DATE 23/6 EXT. INT. X
CAMERAMAN BURNS

Left: The clapper-board consists of two hinged pieces of wood that are brought together sharply at the start of each take. This helps the director and editor to keep the takes in order.

Behind the Screen

Hundreds of other people are involved in the making of a film. Some of them get a credit, some of them don't.

The continuity supervisor certainly hopes that his or her work *won't* be noticed by an audience. If it is noticed, then it must have been done badly. The job involves making sure that each shot of the finished film flows smoothly into the next shot, without any changes of detail unless they are part of the storyline. This is because the different parts of a film are not shot in the order seen in the cinema.

Film critics delight in spotting continuity blunders. For example, during one musical number in *The King and I*, Yul Brunner can be seen wearing an earring in some shots – but not in others. In *Anatomy of a Murder*, Lee Remick is seen in a cafe wearing a dress. When she walks outside, she is suddenly wearing trousers.

Sound and Vision

At least five people normally back up the camera operator. The main job of the focus-puller is to keep the camera in **focus** and to change the lens when necessary. At the other end of the camera, film-stock has to be loaded and taken out. The person who does this is also in charge of the clapperboard, so in the credits this job is usually shown as 'clapper-loader'.

The gaffer is the chief electrician, who works to get the lighting effects required by the cinematographer. The best boy is the gaffer's assistant. Finally, in this group is the key grip, who moves the camera from one position to another and organizes the setting up of rails for smooth **tracking** shots.

Recording the sound-track is also a team effort. On the set are the boom operator and the sound mixer. The boom is a long, adjustable rod with a microphone on the end. The operator moves the boom as necessary, in order to pick up dialogue or other live sound. Care must be taken to avoid dangling the microphone within camera range.

The sound mixer is in charge of the equipment which records sounds picked up by the microphone.

Later, when shooting is finished, the final sound-track is put together by the dubbing editor. As well as the dialogue tracks, there are usually music tracks and sound effects tracks. These have to be blended smoothly by the dubbing mixer into a single track.

Below: *Supergirl*, filmed at Pinewood studios in England, employed one engineering shop, two model workshops and a mechanical special effects unit.

Selling the Film

Between the making of a film and the screening of that film to the cinema audience, there is a process known as distribution. For a fee, or a percentage of the profits, the distributor will try to get the film seen by as large an audience as possible.

One of the first things a distributor has to do is to submit the film to the Board of Film Censors. This Board judges whether the film is fit to be seen by everyone, or whether it is only suitable for older children or adults.

After consideration, the Board issues a certificate – 'U', 'PG', '15' or '18' in Britain. Sometimes a distributor is unhappy about the certificate a film has been given, and agrees to cut out certain scenes in order to get a different rating. *Footloose*, for example, would have been certificated 15, but the distributor cut out a violent scene so that the censor would agree to it being PG. This made it available to a much wider audience.

Another part of the distributor's job is to work out how many prints of the film are going to be needed. Each print costs around £1000 to make. Some films are judged to be of a type that audiences will either want to see immediately or not at all. For such films a 'blanket' release is planned. This means that enough prints have to be made for the film to be shown all over the

Below: An attention-grabbing poster helps to sell the film to the public.

40

country at the same time. For a new James Bond film, as many as 500 prints may be made at the same time for British release.

Finally, before the film opens to the public, the distributor will organize a publicity campaign. Some of this publicity, like posters and advertisements, is very costly. The distributor will also try to get free publicity by persuading TV and radio producers to invite one of the stars onto a chat show.

Often a song is written specifically to promote a film. If this song becomes popular, it brings the film to the attention of millions of people. The record and film of *Ghostbusters* illustrate this very well.

How does Eddie Murphy follow a movie like Trading Places?

Easy

BEVERLY HILLS Cop

15

Going to the Cinema

Going to the cinema is quite a different experience from watching the same film on TV. Apart from the size and clarity of the picture on the screen, sharing a film with the other members of the audience can be a major part of the enjoyment. A comedy seems much funnier when a group of people are laughing together; a thriller becomes more thrilling; a horror film seems safer because the audience can give each other a sense of security.

Ever since the early days of cinema-going, the sale of food and drink has always been important. Many people expect to eat when they go to see a film, whether they are hungry or not. In fact, cinemas depend more on profits from the sale of sweets, hot dogs, ice creams, popcorn and drinks than they do on the sale of admission tickets.

Showing the Film

Above and behind the audience, the film is prepared and shown by the projectionist. When a 35-mm feature film arrives at a cinema it is

Above: A visit to a cinema involves more than just the feature film.

in five or six separate cans. Each can contains 2000 feet (610 m) of film, which will give twenty minutes of screen time. If a film is going to be shown in the same cinema for at least a week, then the projectionist will normally stick all the different reels together, end to end, and transfer the whole film onto one enormous **spool**. This way only one projector is needed and the film won't require much attention while it's running.

If a cinema is going to show the film only once or twice, the projectionist keeps the reels separate, and uses two projectors to keep the film going without a break. So that he or she knows when to get the second projector started, a small black dot is printed in the top right-hand corner of the film near to the end of the reel. The black dot appears on the screen for four frames; that is, one sixth of a second. If the projectionist didn't notice the dot, there would be a break in action between one reel and the next. Audiences would complain,

as it would ruin their concentration and so spoil their enjoyment.

Another common source of annoyance can be the quality of the print. Film gets damaged very easily, and most colour film except Technicolor fades with age. Even when handled carefully, film gets battered and strained by projection. One fault on a projector can scratch every print that runs through it. Good projectionists do what they can to clean up and mend the prints they show, but scratches just won't go away, and missing frames can't be replaced.

Along Came Video

Television and video are normally thought of as being very modern, but in fact they are only thirty years younger than film. In the 1920s, the British inventor John Logie Baird worked on both ideas with some success. He gave a public demonstration of television in 1928, transmitting a picture from London to New York using electronic signals.

At the same time, he developed a brittle plastic video disk which worked in the same way as a record on a record-player. It fitted onto a turntable, which revolved 78 times per minute. When the needle came into contact with the disk, electronic signals were sent to the Baird television receiver to which it was connected and a visual image appeared. The disk produced 12 still images which each stayed on the screen for about fifteen seconds.

TV and Video

For a few years these disks were on sale to the general public. However, the real possibilities of video were not fully explored for another twenty years.

The idea was revived in the fifties because of demand from television companies. At this time, every programme had to be either transmitted live, mistakes and all, or recorded on film, which was very expensive. A cheap video-recording system was urgently needed.

The solution came in 1956. An American company called Ampex produced a system modelled not on disks, but on audio tape.

Above: A picture produced on a receiver by one of Baird's video disks in 1938. It lasted several seconds.

Video tape works in exactly the same way as audio tape. Both are made from plastic film coated with a layer of magnetic particles. If the tape is passed over a **recording head**, the electric signals from the head cause a change in the pattern of the particles. When the tape is played back at the same speed, the recording head 'reads' the magnetic pattern, and so the electronic signals reproduce the original sound and picture it recorded.

However, to record a video image, much more information needs to be stored on tape than when simply recording sound. The Ampex equipment solved this problem by using 2-inch wide (5-cm) tape, and four recording heads instead of one. Furthermore, each of the heads rotated while the tape passed over it. The system produced excellent playback quality, and was in use by television before the year was out.

Good though the Ampex system was, there was room for improvement because it was expensive and heavy. Each machine was about 3 m high, 2 m wide, and 1 m deep. Spools were up to $1\frac{1}{2}$ m wide. What was needed was a system that used narrower

Below: A modern Laser Vision disk. It spins at 18,000 revolutions per minute, and contains 108,000 frames.

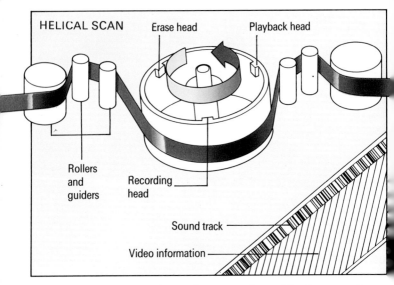

HELICAL SCAN

Erase head

Playback head

Rollers and guiders

Recording head

Sound track

Video information

tape. Once this was achieved, the rest of the equipment could be scaled down too.

At this point, in 1964, the lead was taken by the Japanese company Toshiba. They developed a technique that was originally known as 'slant track' recording – a name that describes it very well. What it means is that the tape passes over the head at a slant, not at a right angle. All the information is laid down in long, slanting tracks, so that 2-inch (5-cm) worth of pictures can be packed onto tape only 1 inch (2·5 cm) wide. The sound is recorded on a strip on one edge of the tape, by a separate recording head.

At first this slant track, or helical scan system as it came to be known, was achieved by having the **supply spool** mounted higher than the **take-up spool**, with the recording head in the middle. The tape then had to pass over the head at an angle.

Later, when tape became even narrower, and small machines were introduced for use in the home, helical scan was achieved by having the head drum leaning over to one side. If you take the cassette out of a home video cassette recorder (VCR) and shine a torch inside the machine, you should be able to see the leaning drum.

Video in TV

The video breakthrough of 1956 completely changed television broadcasting. Suddenly, things which had previously been impossible became easy. As a result, it is fairly rare to see a 'live' broadcast these days.

Playback and Editing
Saturday afternoon sports coverage would seem to be an obvious example of live television, but in fact video is used a great deal in these programmes. Pre-recorded interviews and slow-motion action replays looking from different angles at the way a goal was scored – these would be impossible without video. A live event such as a royal wedding is recorded on video as it goes out, for later playback as an **edited** news item.

The opportunity of editing television programmes was made possible by video. In the days when most programmes went out live, studio plays, panel games

Below: Electronic News Gathering is one of video's latest conquests over film.

and comedy shows often contained various mistakes and blunders. Many over-ran their time and had to be cut off before the end. Now pre-recording and editing make them mistake-free and exactly the right length.

Out and About

The last area of television to be affected by video was the news. Even after helical scanning was invented, video-recording equipment was still too bulky and heavy to be moved around easily. Outside broadcast (OB) vans were able to record some news events, but not all of them. They could only go where there were roads.

During the fifties and sixties, television had to rely on

AN OUTSIDE BROADCAST VAN

1 Power supply
2 Production desk
3 Monitor
4 Twin video tape recorders

5 Other equipment
6 Air conditioning
7 Camera operator
8 Engineer's desk

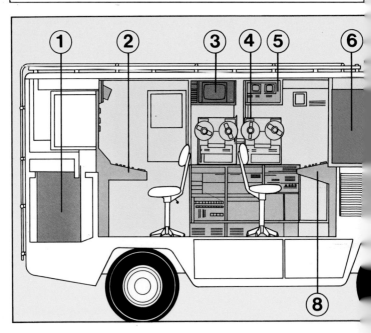

film more than on video for recording unscheduled news events. Film cameras, being portable, could reach places that video cameras could not get near. The disadvantage of this situation was that film needed to be physically carried back to the studio, and chemically processed. This resulted in a delay of several hours before it could be shown on television.

All this changed in the 1970s, when Sony invented the U-Matic video format. This used tape only $\frac{3}{4}$ inches (2 cm) wide, inside a cassette. When used with a light-weight camera, U-Matic video recording was able to take over from film. This system is known as ENG (electronic news gathering), and it does not need to be either processed or transported. Instead, it can simply be electronically transmitted back to the studio (or sent by satellite from one country to another) within a matter of seconds. ENG is also cheaper, because it needs fewer operators than film.

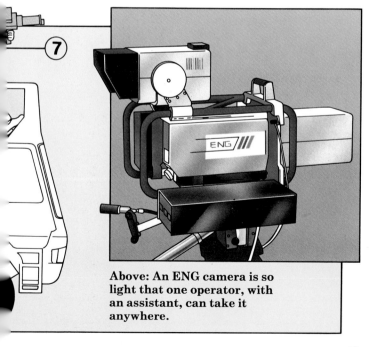

Above: An ENG camera is so light that one operator, with an assistant, can take it anywhere.

Rock Videos

Most rock videos make use of both film and video.

Normally, the material is **storyboarded**, then shot on 35-mm film. Everything is shot several times, with different camera-angles, backgrounds, lighting, and performances. This is likely to use up around one hour of film, which will have to be edited down to about three minutes, to fit the song.

One way of doing this is to copy it from film onto videotape. This process is known as **telecine transfer**. Using a video editing suite, the job of cutting and re-arranging the different parts can then be done quickly and cleanly.

Special Powers

Once it has been edited, other **post-production** work can also be done on video.

For example, the video for Michael Jackson's record *Billie Jean* was based on the idea of him having special powers. Paving slabs were made to light up as he stepped on them. Figures in adverts became animated, in time with his singing. Special effects such as these are usually added at post-production stage.

Most videos are made in a few days, at a cost of around £10,000. However, a few superstars have spent more money in an attempt to produce something special. The longest, the most ambitious and the most expensive video yet made is Michael Jackson's *Thriller*. Unlike most videos, this was not produced quickly just to help sell a record. In fact, the

song was already world-famous before the video was made.

Jackson hired a top director, top make-up artist and top dance-arranger to work with him on the project. He chose John Landis to direct, and Rick Baker to do the make-up, because he had seen and admired their work on the feature-film *An American Werewolf in London*. The new techniques of **animatronics** (described in chapter 7) were used, as well as make-up and masks, to transform him into a man-panther. The result, shot and edited on film, lasted fourteen minutes. It has played in some cinemas as a short film, as well as achieving international acclaim as a video.

Powerful Promotion
The number of rock videos produced each year

Below: Michael Jackson's *Thriller* – not so much a pop 'promo' as a mini-film.

approaches 3000. About 1500 of these are made in America. In the UK the total is about 1000; France and Germany make about 100 each.

Record companies are always trying to pack their three-minute videos with enough originality and technical brilliance to make a lasting impact. This is because the aim of most rock videos is to promote and sell the record they accompany. What producers want most of all is for their video 'promos' to be played on MTV, the American non-stop rock-video TV channel, and on the BBC's *Top of the Pops*.

Video in the Clubs

However, television is not the only possible outlet for rock videos. In certain pubs and clubs around the country there are now 'video juke boxes'. After putting the right amount of money into a slot, a customer can choose a video, which is then played automatically. Discos are another outlet for videos as well as records. This could mean that DJs will be gradually replaced by VJs.

Below: The futuristic fantasy of Duran Duran's award-winning *Wild Boys* video.

Video in Film-making

Another professional area where film and video sometimes work side-by-side is that of feature film-making. Film producers are always eager to cut costs, and where video offers a way of saving time and money, the opportunity is likely to be grasped.

Instant Rushes

For more than sixty years, a film director's working day has normally begun with watching the 'rushes'. These are the prints taken from the film-stock that was passed through the cameras the day before. The director has to be satisfied that some of the **takes** are good enough for the final print. If, as sometimes happens, none of the takes have worked very well, then the director has to re-stage and re-shoot the entire scene.

Obviously, setting everything up again is a lengthy and therefore costly operation.

To avoid the extra cost, directors working on big productions record on film and video at the same time. Within minutes of a scene being staged and filmed, the director can look at it on video and decide whether the film take is going to be satisfactory when printed. If it is not, then the scene can be re-shot straightaway, while everything is set up.

A similar use can be made of video when a particular effect needs to be added to the film at a later stage. In *The Company of Wolves*, for example, the script called for a wolf's head to be chopped off, and for this action to be shown in slow motion. Video was used by the film unit to

Right: Shooting on video provides instant 'rushes' for the director's guidance.

check on whether their head-chopping sequence was going to look effective when slowed down.

Feedback for Monsters

There is another way in which the small screen is used in the service of the big screen. This happens during the making of films in which people have to operate puppets or monsters, or other non-humans. During the filming of *The Dark Crystal*, the puppeteers operating characters called Jen and Kira were hidden underneath the stage, except for their hands. In order to see their own hands 'acting', and to avoid bumping into each other, the puppeteers had small TV screens showing them live pictures from the stage.

Similarly, in *Return to Oz*, the actor inside Tik-Tok, a character made up mainly of a large metal sphere, had to walk backwards, bent over double. In order to see where he was going he had a tiny TV inside his costume.

Below: Using a telecine transfer unit, programmes shot on film may be transferred to video for ease of playback.

Video Comes Home

It is only recently that video has become cheap and convenient enough for use in the home. Toshiba brought out a $\frac{1}{2}$ inch (1.3 cm) system intended for this purpose as early as 1964, but it never became very popular. The reason for its lack of success was that it was based on the reel-to-reel system, which meant that people had to handle the tape themselves and thread it through a fairly tricky path on a slant.

Home video successfully arrived in 1972, when Sony devised its $\frac{3}{4}$-inch (2-cm) U-Matic system. Using a cassette that slipped easily into the recorder, it was no longer necessary for the user to touch the tape at all. A few months later, $\frac{1}{2}$-inch (1.3-cm) cassette systems were available at reasonable prices, and the home video boom began. Within 13 years, 45% of homes in the UK had video. In North America the

55

figure is lower – 34% – but increasing rapidly. In France the figure is around 17%.

One of the main uses of home video cassette recorders (VCRs) is 'time-shift viewing'. People can record a programme which they want to watch, but which is on at an inconvenient time, and watch it later on. If there are two programmes which they want to watch being transmitted at the same time, they can simply record one while watching the other. And most VCRs have a timer device which allows people to record their favourite programmes even if they go away for several days.

Videograms (pre-recorded video cassettes) are now available from thousands of high street video shops. Usually you need to take out membership after which you can rent a videogram overnight, or longer, for a pound or two.

Below: Inside a video cassette recorder.

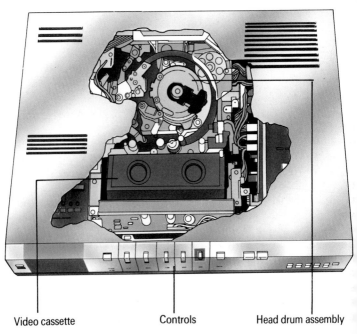

Video cassette   Controls   Head drum assembly

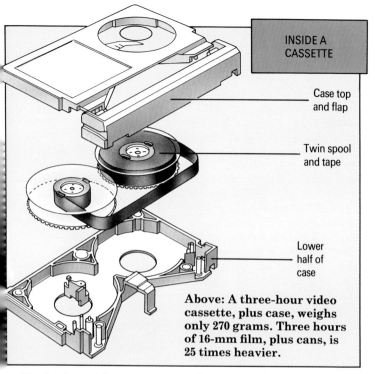

INSIDE A
CASSETTE

Case top
and flap

Twin spool
and tape

Lower
half of
case

**Above: A three-hour video
cassette, plus case, weighs
only 270 grams. Three hours
of 16-mm film, plus cans, is
25 times heavier.**

To begin with, the only type of material available on videograms were full-length feature films. Films can go on offer on video within a year of their cinema release.

The range has now broadened, however, and there are other types of videogram that can be rented or bought. These are mainly how-to-do-it tapes. For sports fans, there are tapes about diving, tennis, board-sailing, squash, cricket, badminton, and many others. For example, if you want to study closely how someone serves in tennis, then the replay and **freeze-frame** facilities on a VCR can be very useful.

Other tapes include Chinese cookery, learning a foreign language, keep-fit, self-defence, yoga, passing a driving test, training dogs pottery, exam revision and growing vegetables.

One recent development is that you can now borrow videograms from some public libraries, just like a book or a record. However, videogram-borrowing is not free.

The Video World

As well as being used in film and TV, video has spread into many other areas of life. In schools, offices, hospitals and shops, video provides a means of information and education. Progress has been so rapid that many new ideas, such as video telephones, may soon become a reality.

In many modern supermarkets you are likely to see notices which say 'Video-recording is in operation in this store'. Cameras constantly survey shoppers as they take goods from the shelves. If store detectives suspect someone of stealing, video may provide evidence.

Similarly, in the event of a bank robbery, staff can set off a video camera by touching a foot-switch.

Video Training

Sales assistants, teachers, gymnasts, actors – all these people, and many more, can improve their performance

by the use of video recordings. Some fire brigades now use video to make an on-the-spot record of fires, and of the way each fire is tackled. Such videotapes are later used for training purposes. New members can learn a great deal about fire-fighting from watching the videos, and also about other brigade services such as cliff rescue.

New recruits to the staff of the big supermarkets and department stores are often

Left: Cameras in a U.S. bank dramatically captured this thief's attempt to shoot them out of action.

Above: Slow-motion replay gives athletes some useful ideas of how to improve their performance.

shown specially-made ten-minute programmes on such topics as 'Using the Till' and 'Payment by Cheque'. Training managers find that these tapes help new staff far more than lecturing used to.

In some cases, people can benefit from watching themselves in action. A gymnast or fencer, for example, may want to study his or her movements and work out how to improve them. Slow-motion is very helpful here.

59

The Giant Screen

Video and TV displays are no longer confined to small indoor screens. Since 1980, it has been possible to get a bright, easily-seen image onto a giant screen even in glaring sunlight.

This system was pioneered by the Mitsubishi Corporation in Japan. Instead of using just one **electron beam tube**, like a home TV set, their DiamondVision screen may contain as many as 150,000 tubes. These give out such brightness that it is

best for a viewer to be at least 50 metres away.

The exact size and shape of these screens varies according to what sort of pictures are going to be shown on them. For rugby, cricket, football and baseball, screens of about 8 m high and 10 m wide are common. For horse-racing, however, a viewer needs a more 'Cinemascope' shaped screen.

The images shown on the screen can come from a number of sources. Mos

interviews with some of the players, recorded highlights from some previous matches, a selection of new rock videos and old cartoons to fill up the time. During the match itself, video can be used to provide action replay of exciting moments – as in broadcast TV.

Video Concerts

However, sports events are not the only users of giant screens. The 1985 *Live Aid* rock concerts that took place at the same time in London and Philadelphia both had DiamondVision screens in the huge stadiums. Without them, thousands of the fans there would have had difficulty in seeing anything at all. Live pictures were also beamed by satellite from the London stage to the Philadelphia screen, and vice versa.

At a rock concert, unlike a sporting event, the action is more or less fixed in one place – the stage. The camera-operators can be positioned very close to the band, maybe just below the level of the stage. Also, ENG equipment is so light that they can move around the stage itself getting side-views and rear-views of the performance.

Above: Top rock musicians often play in huge stadiums. Without the giant screen, most fans would hardly be able to see the stage.

commonly, they come live from ENG cameras operated within the stadium itself. For a sports event the cameras obviously have to keep out of the way of the action, so the operators work from a distance.

Pre-recorded videotape can also be used as a means of extra entertainment at a sports event. Before a match starts there may be taped

61

The Video Watchdog

The rise of video has provided the police with a powerful tool. Their cameras are used as part of a closed-circuit television (CCTV) set-up. This means that the cameras transmit pictures which are watched live in the control room. Later, if necessary, the police can watch the pictures again on video.

Police use CCTV regularly at football grounds. The cameras, operated by **remote control**, constantly observe parts of the ground where the police think that trouble might start. In this way one person watching several screens in the control room can survey the whole ground. The cameras, being high up, can see far more than officers on foot could.

Zooming In
When it looks as if violence is breaking out somewhere, a camera lens **zooms in** for closer inspection. If necessary, officers around the ground are contacted by radio. An arrest might be made, in which case the video-recording would later be shown in court as evidence.

Because of this possibility, all police video cameras are fitted with a mechanism which constantly keeps the date and the time showing in a corner of the picture. If they didn't do this, video pictures would be useless as evidence.

Eye in the Sky
Another kind of crowd that the police sometimes feel it necessary to keep an eye on is the protest march, or demonstration. When people

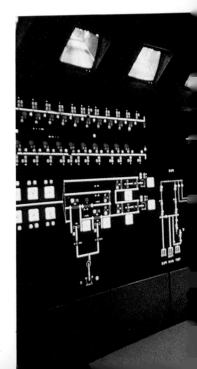

are on the move, the type of fixed cameras used in football grounds are not much use. In this situation, the police sometimes use a camera operated from within a helicopter. They refer to this as 'an eye in the sky'. This eye keeps a look-out for people who have collapsed, as well as for possible trouble.

A Motorway Monitor

Motorways also come in for attention from police cameras. A video system linked to a computer helps police spot stolen cars. The camera is fixed to a motorway bridge, and aimed so that it can see car number-plates as they pass under. With the help of the computer, it not only sees them: it also 'reads' them. The computer then checks every registration number to see whether it belongs to a car that is listed as lost or stolen. This does not mean that the police recover such vehicles instantly, but it does put them on the track.

Below: CCTV screens allow a single controller to survey a vast amount of traffic.

Doing It Yourself

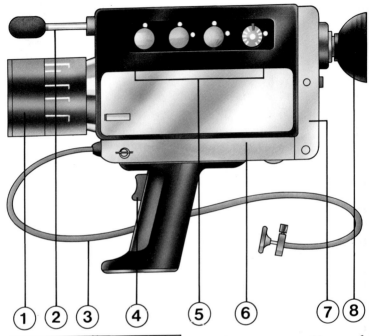

① ② ③ ④ ⑤ ⑥ ⑦ ⑧

THE SUPER-8 CAMERA

1 Zoom lens
2 Microphone
3 Cable release for stop-
  frame work
4 Grip and trigger
5 Control panel
6 Battery compartment
7 Cassette
  compartment
8 Adjustable eyepiece

Making your own films and videos is an expensive hobby. The best way for young enthusiasts to start is to join a school or youth club's film or video society.

Super-8

In 1965, Kodak introduced an amateur film-making system based on 8-mm film housed inside a cassette. Super-8, as it is called, proved much simpler to use than previous

64

systems. With a **sound stripe** added in 1972, Super-8 is now a well-tried, reasonably cheap, movie-making system.

With modern Super-8 equipment, you can film more or less anything. The essential difference between 8-mm film and the 35-mm film in professional use is to do with projection. You can't satisfactorily project 8-mm film across a large public hall. But for showing at home, or in a classroom, it's fine.

Getting Started

To start filming with a Super-8 camera, all you need is a suitable subject and reasonably bright light. The actual operating instructions are set out in a number of books and magazines, that offer detailed guidance on Super-8 movie-making. Schools, youth clubs and community centres sometimes set up Super-8 clubs.

When the film has been processed you will need a Super-8 projector, which laces the film automatically.

Right: This animation was produced very quickly and simply by children, drawing directly onto clear 35-mm film with spirit-based pens.

Later, as you get more ambitious, other items of equipment, such as a **cutter** and a **splicer**, for editing, become desirable.

Film Societies

Production is not the only side of film-making that need not be left entirely to professionals. Screening can also be done on an amateur basis. The film size suitable for amateur film-screening is 16-mm. Using 16-mm, you can project a fairly big image that will be seen clearly by 100 or more people.

Many schools, youth clubs and community centres own a 16-mm projector. It is not as easy to operate as an 8-mm projector, because each reel has to be laced up by hand. However, teachers and youth club leaders have sometimes been trained to do this, and have acquired a certificate.

There are hundreds of film societies showing films all over the country. The seating and print quality are rarely as good as those in a cinema, but members have

Below: For film societies there are thousands of 16-mm films to choose from many different countries. Just reading the catalogues can be fun.

SCHOOL FILM SOCIETY

This month's films:

ORPHÉE — 7.30
PSYCHO — 8.30
ALEXANDER NEVSKY — 7.3
INTOLERANCE —
LES ENFANTS DU PARADIS — 5.00 FRIDAY

16mm FILM ★
Catalogue

Films for Hire

he luxury of choosing the films they want to see, when they want to see them.

Films on Offer

There are over 8000 feature films for societies to choose from. These range from silent comedies of the twenties to space fantasies of the eighties. As well as British and American films, there are films made in many other countries all around the world.

On top of all these features, there are thousands of short films. These offer an even greater variety of style and subject than the features too. This is because a lot of them have been made not by

Above: *Jobs for the Girls*, made by the Sheffield Film Co-op, is an independent film about a young woman who wants to be a motorcycle mechanic.

the big studios, but independently. A short film made in this way can be original and adventurous. It can even make fun of the big studios' output. A short film called *Hardware Wars*, for example, sends up the *Star Wars* blockbusters.

Other short films listed in the catalogues include **animation**, documentaries, experimental films, and films from the 1890s by such pioneers as Méliès and the Lumière brothers.

67

The Camcorder

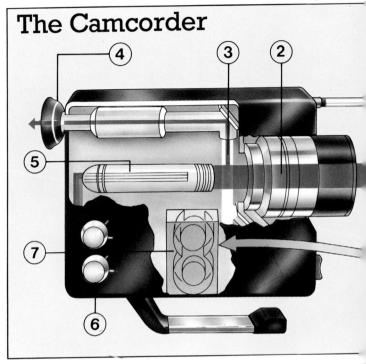

Even after the invention of the $\frac{3}{4}$-inch (2-cm) U-Matic cassette system, video cameras were much too expensive for most people to even think of owning one. Furthermore, there were too many things that could go wrong, and they were heavy.

Various lighter and simpler systems were developed. The most recent is the camcorder. As its name suggests, this combines a camera with a recorder. A typical camcorder weighs about five pounds and produces cassettes tha can be played back on ar ordinary home VCR. It car take power either from bat teries or from the mains.

With a camcorder, hom movies are easier to make than ever before. Film wa usually used for specia occasions, but the camcor der's cheapness and simplic ity mean that everyday family activities can b recorded at great length Probably no-one outside th family will be in the least bi

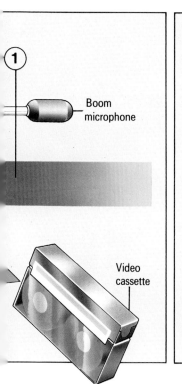

Boom microphone

Video cassette

Light (1) from the subject being recorded passes through the lens-barrel (2), to the 'beamsplitter' (3). From here, a section of the beam of light is sent to the eyepiece (4). By this means, the user sees exactly what the lens is seeing, even though the eyepiece is higher up. The rest of the light beam goes through a 'saticon tube' (5), which breaks it up into its three colours – red, blue and green. After adjustment by the controls (6), the image is recorded on a mini-cassette (7). Sound from all directions is recorded by the microphone, which is on a boom so that it can get close to the main subject.

nterested in watching the playback, but for a home movie that doesn't matter.

Camcorder or Super-8?

In some areas the camcorder has obvious advantages over Super-8. It can record continuously for at least an hour; no time or money need be spent in processing, and it uses a TV screen that's already in the home.

However, whereas film editing can be done quite successfully at home with the right equipment, smooth video editing can be done only with a costly professional suite. At home, a rough job can be done by borrowing someone else's VCR, linking the two together, and transferring selected shots from one to the other. This is known as 'crash-editing', and is jumpy and messy to watch.

For the dramatic effects that can be achieved by editing, Super-8 still has the edge over a camcorder.

Video Workshops

Video workshops have sprung up all over the country. Each workshop consists of a small group of people who work on independent video productions. Sometimes, at weekends and during school holidays, they run courses for young people.

The aim of such a course is to provide first-hand experience of video – not to produce masterpieces.

Typically, it will start with a course on how to operate the equipment. Then there is a discussion of ideas for filming, and possible subjects

Above: Video can easily be taken out and about; for example, to get opinions and comments from a person in the street.

to work on. Finally a plan i produced, and the youn people start shooting.

Youth clubs and school use video in many differen ways. One fairly commo approach is to stage a job interview, and make a vide recording of it. This not onl gives young people a chanc to operate cameras, but als allows them, on playback, t see themselves as a prospe tive employer would.

Video Scratching

'Video scratching' involves mixing together an assortment of television pictures with a new soundtrack. The simplest way of going about it is to connect an audio cassette player to a VCR. Play a music tape, set the VCR recording, then switch from one channel to another repeatedly, in time with the music. You might get bits of a soap opera, a wildlife documentary, animation, and a political interview. The music replaces the original soundtrack, and binds the assorted clips together. A rather more complicated technique uses two connected VCRs. On one tape is a store of carefully-chosen clips, that may have been collected over a long period of time. Particular items, selected because they suit the music or the words of the song, are then transferred to another video-tape. In between the pictures a fuzzy screen will appear – but then scratch video isn't meant to look like smoothly-edited film.

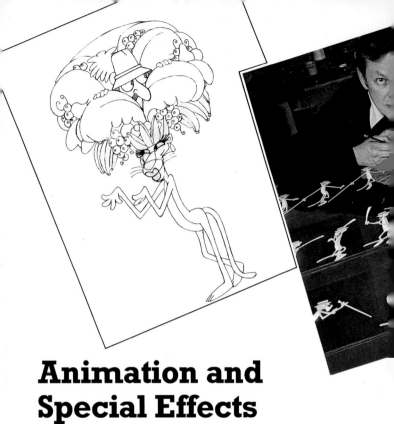

Animation and Special Effects

Some of the most famous film stars have been drawings and models. King Kong, Mickey Mouse, Bugs Bunny, the Pink Panther – these and others have brought pleasure to millions. To create them, however, has become increasingly expensive, so computers have begun to replace human hands.

24 Pink Panthers a Second
Animation is based on the fact that all films are made up of still pictures.

In traditional animation, photographs are taken of a series of drawings. Each drawing is very slightly different to the one before it, so that when they are projected the characters or object appear to move (become 'animated'). The drawing are done on separate sheet

72

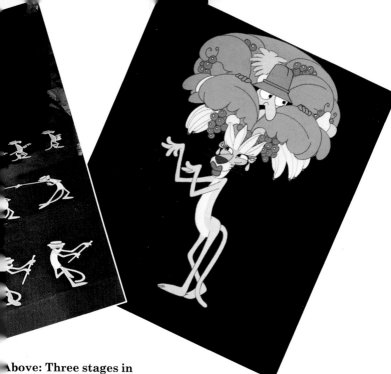

Above: Three stages in creating a Pink Panther cartoon. The original sketch is drawn onto 'cels', then photographed onto film.

f transparent film, called cels'. Since film is projected t 24 frames per second, 24 rawings are needed in order o create one second of creen time.

Disney Magic

he most famous creator of nimated films was Walt isney. His animators put ast amounts of detail into heir drawings, so that leaves rustled in the breeze, transparent drops of water splashed in ponds, and reflections and shadows were used to dramatic effect. Using this approach it took Disney four years to produce *Snow White and the Seven Dwarfs*.

Over the last thirty years, Disney's style of full animation has become too expensive – even for Disney. Cartoons produced for television have resorted to half-animation, with flat, unchanging backgrounds and repetitive movements.

73

Model FX

Special effects (FX) are used when it is impossible to stage something in front of the cameras for real. Animation is regarded as being a special effect when it is seen in the same frame as live action.

This kind of special effect is usually provided by models rather than a series of drawings. Model animation works in basically the same way as drawn animation. **Stop-frame** photography takes a series of still pictures, with the action in each frame being slightly advanced on the one before. However, the animator does not have to make a new model for each frame. Instead, the model is made flexible enough to be used again and again, with the position of the limbs or body being altered from shot to shot.

A Sympathetic Monster

The most famous example of model animation is still King Kong, even after more than fifty years. The giant ape who

74

struck terror and pity into the hearts of millions of cinema-goers was in reality a little aluminium skeleton, covered in rubber, cotton, latex and rabbit fur.

His creator was a man named Willis O'Brien. O'Brien's particular achievement lay in making Kong into a real character, not just a roaring monster. He gave Kong mannerisms, facial expressions and moving eyes.

A variety of methods were used to make Kong seem about sixty feet tall, while appearing in the same settings as the actors. In some shots, the size of everything else in the frame – huts, trees, the Empire State Building – was scaled down. Even the human heroine was replaced by a four-inch model at times. For other shots, another Kong was built at full-size – but only his head and shoulders, and one paw. The result was very convincing, and the film made a fortune.

Skeletons and Snakes

O'Brien's methods have been developed over the years by one of his assistants – Ray Harryhausen. In *Jason and the Argonauts* for example, Harryhausen animated a famous sequence in which Jason fights seven skeleton-warriors. This was an extremely complicated job, because each skeleton had four limbs and a head. That meant that for each frame, thirty-five different parts had to be moved.

However, most producers now consider it to be too expensive, and are turning to electronics as a cheaper alternative.

Above: For certain scenes, a full-scale model of Kong's head and shoulders was built. There was also a wire-operated paw.

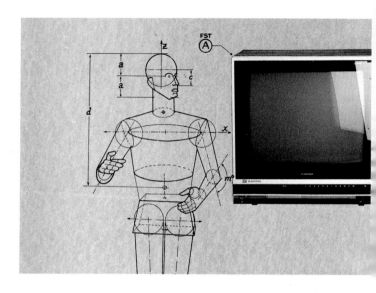

Video Animation

Until very recently, smooth frame-by-frame animation was impossible with video. Now, a **single-frame** $\frac{1}{2}$-inch (1.3-cm) video system is available. It has by no means replaced film in animation, but it is becoming a useful assistant.

As a learning aid it allows students to quickly rough out a series of drawings, tape them frame-by-frame, and watch them on playback to see whether they 'come to life' properly.

This process of trying out drawings by putting them onto video is known as a line test. Experienced animators find line tests just as useful as students. Before single frame video was available they used to have to test their work by flipping through their drawings like a flicker book.

Add a Computer

Computers have opened up all sorts of possibilities for the animator.

Computers can think only in terms of numbers, so the drawing has to be **digitized** (changed into numbers) before the computer can do anything with it. This is done

Left: Traditional line animation is still the most popular choice, even when a hi-tech, computerized look is needed.

either by sending instructions to the computer screen via a keyboard, or by drawing in an outline with a special pen onto an electronic pad linked to the computer.

Various instructions can then be sent to make changes to the drawing on the screen. These include 'squash', 'stretch', 'wobble', 'bend', 'twist', 'spiral' and 'explode'.

For animators, adding a computer memory also means that line testing can be done in a much more sophisticated way than with just a camera and recorder. Once a sequence is stored in the computer's memory, it can be replayed at any speed. Individual frames can be duplicated, added in, taken out, or changed around. Professional animators are very keen on this type of assistance, even when they feel limited by the lifelessness of the computer's other routines.

Below: Max Headroom, smooth-talking presenter of his own TV rock video show, was brought to life by altering an actor's features by computer animation.

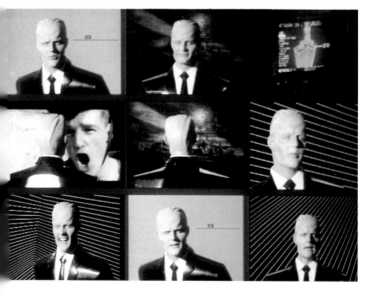

Computers and the Cinema

New technology in the eighties helped to produce *Tron* and *The Last Starfighter*, two feature films which used a lot of computer animation. There is nothing much in either of the films that could not have been produced by conventional animation methods. The difference is that these methods would have taken twenty times longer.

Computer Starfighters

Frames of film that have been produced by computer can vary in quality, depending on the number of polygons in them. A polygon is the smallest possible detail from which the picture is made up. Even in the two years between *Tron* and *The Last Starfighter* there was a major change in computer powers. In *Tron* there were never more than 30,000 polygons in any one frame. For *The Last Starfighter*, using a CRAY X-MP, the most powerful computer in the world at that time, the animators were able to compose frames that contained an average of one

million polygons. This resulted in a much smoother picture.

Because of this, the images in *Tron* look 'computerized' – as they are meant to, because the action takes place inside the mind of a computer. In *The Last Starfighter*, however, they are meant to look like real objects.

Right: One of the computerized sequences from *Tron*.

In-betweening

A further advance between the two films was the time it took to produce each frame of animated film.

After the artwork had been digitized, programmers gave the computer the key frames. These show the position of all the objects at the main points of the action. The computer was then told to 'in-between' – to draw in all the frames needed to take the action from one key frame to the next stage in the action.

For the animated sequences in *Tron*, the computer took an average of five minutes to produce each in-between frame. For *The Last Starfighter*, this job had been reduced to an average of two minutes. Even so, it meant that each second of screen time took at least 48 minutes to create.

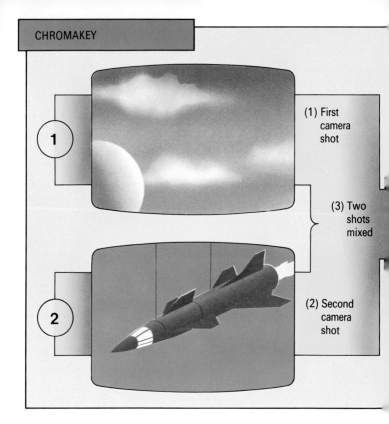

(1) First camera shot

(3) Two shots mixed

(2) Second camera shot

Video FX

Television studios now have a vast range of electronic effects available to them. Some of these, unlike film effects, are not meant to go unnoticed. When a presenter is suddenly picked up, enclosed within a small box, and sent whirling round, or when one scene changes to another by means of being turned over like a page in a book – such effects are part of the entertainment.

A completely different type of video effect, achieved by a device known as chromakey, is *not* brought to the attention of the viewer, however. Chromakey is a method of combining a person or object from one place,

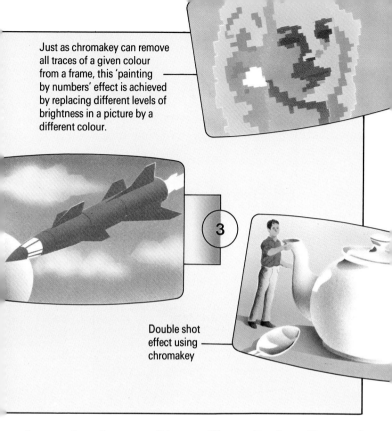

Just as chromakey can remove all traces of a given colour from a frame, this 'painting by numbers' effect is achieved by replacing different levels of brightness in a picture by a different colour.

3

Double shot effect using chromakey

and a setting from another into a single image.

The person or object to be 'transported' must be in front of a blue background. Blue is chosen because it is almost entirely absent from human skin colouring. The chromakey then removes all blue from the frame. All that remains in the frame is the person or object. The missing background is then replaced by an appropriate scene.

Chromakey has all sorts of dramatic uses. For example, it can make someone appear to be very small, without the expense of building over-size props. This is done by filming the person from a long distance with one camera, while the other camera shows the setting, perhaps a forest, in close-up. In this way, when the two pictures are merged, the person may seem to be no bigger than a flower.

Animatronics

When Rick Baker was given the first-ever Make-Up Oscar in 1982, he had in fact branched out beyond make-up into what is now known as animatronics.

For a long time, Baker and John Landis, the director, had wanted to make a film in which a man would change into a werewolf before the audience's very eyes, during a continuous take. Previously such transformations had been done by dissolves – one stage of the transformation fading into the next, and so on.

At first, Baker and Landis did not know how their idea could be achieved. Nothing like it had ever been done before.

It was not until an invention called 'Smooth-on' became available that the idea became a real possibility. Flesh-like in appearance, like foam-rubber but far more elastic, Smooth-on was used to show the actor's hand growing into a wolf-claw.

The actor's real hand was kept out of camera range. The hand that changed was a construction full of cables and plastic tubing, covered over with Smooth-on. The cables, rather like brake-cables on a bike, went inside the fingers so that operators could make them move. The tubing provided the 'growth'.

Right: Animatronics in action in *An American Werewolf in London*. The actor's real hand is below the frame, out of sight.

Inside each end of the tubing was a syringe, the one at the operator's end being much larger than the one inside the palm. When the operator forced the large plunger down, air-pressure travelled through the tubing and pushed the smaller plunger outwards. The elasticity of the Smooth-on absorbed this force without breaking, and so the hand was able to 'grow' into a claw.

Such techniques as these, and other similar ones, have been used fairly extensively in recent films. *Greystoke*, *Starman* and *The Company of Wolves* have all used some form of animatronics.

As it happens, the Oscar definition of 'Make-up' has now been changed so as to exclude animatronic effects. If Rick Baker wants to win another Oscar, he'll have to go back to paint and wigs.

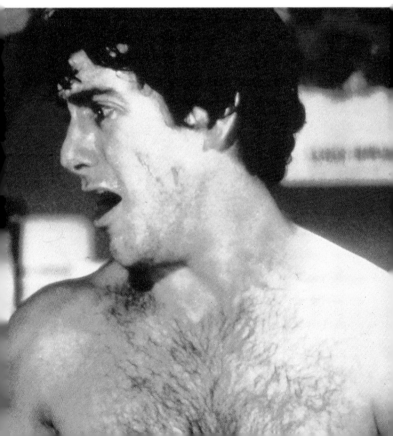

Light and Magic

Many recent blockbusters
owe a great deal of their
success to a Californian company called Industrial Light
and Magic (ILM). It is a film
studio – but actors never
work there. Its job is to bring
to life creatures and effects
that are barely imaginable.

To do this, it will use any
technology, old or new. It is
the special effects capital of
the world.

ILM specializes in making
its effects look completely
realistic. For this purpose,
they have developed some
new approaches. One of

Left: Some shots from *Return of the Jedi* used 63 different model spaceships. The final print composited 170 separate pieces of film. It tooks weeks to do, but lasts only two seconds on the screen.

frames per second, will be just a little blurred round the edges, and therefore more realistic. The speeder-bike sequence in *Return of the Jedi* was mainly created in this way.

Another speciality of ILM involves 'compositing' – that is, bringing together all sorts of images from various sources. The mine-train chase in *Indiana Jones and the Temple of Doom* consisted of model work created at ILM, live action **footage** shot thousands of miles away in London and line animation of flying sparks. At ILM these three sources were edited together in a single image.

Even more complicated was the compositing used in the space battle sequences of the *Stars Wars* films. All the space-craft seen in the finished version had to be controlled and photographed individually. One scene, in *Return of the Jedi*, is the most complicated special FX shot ever achieved.

these is called 'Go-motion'. It works just like stop-frame, except that each frame of film is exposed to light for one full second, rather than for 1/48th of a second as is normal. The idea is that if the film is exposed for a whole second, the object being photographed will shake slightly. The result, when projected at the normal 24

Things to Come

Film and video, as we have seen, are sometimes rivals and sometimes partners. Now that video projection systems and large high-quality TV screens are being developed, video seems all set to invade the cinemas. Meanwhile, both film and video, linked with computers, are exploring new avenues of education and entertainment.

Projecting videotape onto a cinema-size screen became possible in the late seventies. The basic idea involves three separate 'guns', each projecting one of the primary colours – red, blue and green. When they hit the screen, these colours combine to recreate the video picture.

The quality of these enlarged TV pictures varies from system to system, and from tape to tape. Public response has been varied. Some people find them too fuzzy and faint under any circumstances. Other people believe that the best quality video tapes provide a projected image as good as (but not

better than) 16-mm film. A few 'video cinemas' have come into operation. For cinema managers, video offers a major advantage over film: it does away with the expense of employing a projectionist, since anyone can slot a cassette into a VCR.

The World's Largest Television

At the Tokyo Science Expo '85, the Sony Corporation displayed new advances both in screen-size and in picture-quality. These are combined in the Sony Jumbotron, the largest TV screen in the world. It is forty metres wide, and twenty-five metres high. That makes its total surface area more than three times as great as that of an IMAX screen. According to Sony, the Jumbotron can produce a clearer image than any home TV set.

It seems unlikely that Jumbotron screens will be installed very widely, except in sports stadiums and at racetracks. For theatrical entertainment they are simply too big and expensive.

Left: In some cafés and nightclubs, sport and rock videos are now projected as background entertainment.

Below: A Rank Hi-Beam video projector, showing the three separate colour-guns.

It does, however, indicate that high-quality video pictures on a cinema screen are not far off. Whether the experience they will offer an audience can compare with 70-mm film or IMAX remains to be seen.

Future animation

In the field of computer animation, programmers hope to become as good at animating pictures of living things as they are at machinery. For this, they will need a computer with a certain level of artificial intelligence.

87

**Above: In *Star Wars*,
Princess Leia sends a
hologram of herself to Obi
Wan Kenobi in a plea for
help.**

Disks and Lasers

For the home, videograms
are once again available in
plastic disk form. On its
spiral track, a video disk
contains digitalized picture
and sound information.
When the disk is spun at 1800
revolutions per minute, a
diamond or sapphire **stylus**
'reads' the information and
turns it into pictures and
sound.

A video disk has various
advantages compared to
tape. The picture and sound
quality are higher; it is
cheaper, and lasts longer; it
is possible to get fairly quickly from one part of the
recording to another. However, it cannot be used for
recording, and it needs its
own special screen.

Another playback-only
system, called LaserVision,
has a plastic disk coated with
a shiny metallized layer. The
picture-information is read
not by a stylus but by a very
narrow laser beam.

When linked to a com-
puter, LaserVision is ideal
for educational purposes.
The computer knows what is
on each of the 108,000 frames
on a one-hour disk, and any

frame or sequence can be found within seconds and held for as long as it is wanted.

Holograms and 3–D TV

When used with film, lasers can also produce three-dimensional images known as holograms. Holograms are created by splitting a laser beam down the middle. One half of the beam is directed at the film. The other half of the beam strikes the object, then is reflected off onto the film. When the film is illuminated by laser-light, the image is recreated with depth as well as width and height. The future development of holography, linked with computer-control, offers the possibility of genuine 3–D cinema and television.

Some experts predict that in the next century both film and video will have been completely replaced by computers and digital recording. Whether that's true or not, they both have plenty of life left in them at the moment.

Below: In the near future, 3-D TV, which does not require the viewer to wear special glasses, may be successfully developed.

Glossary

Animation Making drawings and models appear to have life.

Animatronics The art of making things seem to live, or grow, by means of electronics and modern chemical substances.

Audio To do with sound and hearing.

Credits Information about who has done what in the making of a particular film.

Cutter A device for cutting a piece of film cleanly, at the required point.

Deep focus lens A particular type of lens which can see things clearly both in the background and in the foreground at the same time.

Digitized Described in terms of numbers, so that a computer can understand.

Dissolve When one film image fades into a different one, so that for a short time both images can be seen on the screen together.

Documentary A type of film that shows events that occur naturally; events that have not been staged specially for the camera's benefit.

Editing The process of cutting out or re-arranging various parts of the material that has been recorded.

Electron The smallest component of matter.

Electron beam tube A glass tube inside which a stream of electrons moves in a vacuum.

Exposure The time needed for the image to be satisfactorily recorded.

Film-stock The actual rolls of plastic that make up film.

Focus A control on a camera which, by moving the lens, enables the operator to see the main subject clearly, without any blurred edges.

Footage A certain length of exposed film.

Frame One complete picture on a piece of film or video.

Freeze-frame A control mechanism on a VCR, which allows the operator to look closely at one particular frame.

High-definition Extremely clear and bright, with no fuzzy edges.

Lace To thread a film correctly through a projector, from one spool to another, so that it is ready to be projected.

Lens A circle of glass or plastic, thicker in the middle than at the edges. It bends beams of light and so controls the way a camera 'sees'.

Limelight A brilliant white light produced by heating a piece of lime.

Post-production The work that is done on a piece of film or video after the actual recording or taping is finished.

Print Film-stock that has been exposed and processed.

Projection When an image is thrown on to a screen as a result of a beam of light passing through a piece of film or glass slide.

Recording head That part of a VCR at which the picture information is actually transferred to or from the tape.

Remote control Command over a machine's operation by means of signals sent from a distance.

Shutter A device that keeps light out of a camera. For a photograph to be taken, the shutter has to be quickly removed and replaced.

Single-frame The same as stop-frame.

Sound stripe A magnetized strip running along the edge of a roll of film. Sound can be recorded on to it, and it then becomes the sound-track.

Splicer A device that makes it possible to stick pieces of film together smoothly and accurately.

Spool A circular framework, made of plastic or metal, which keeps the film tightly rolled.

Stop-frame A technique widely used in animation. It consists of exposing only one frame at a time, and altering the drawing or model between each frame.

Storyboard A plan that shows, by means of drawings, the key scenes of the material to be shot.

Stylus A tiny piece of diamond or sapphire which follows the groove on a disk.

Supply spool The spool which the tape is on at the start of recording or playback.

Synchronized Organized so that two or more things happen at the same time; for instance in film, when the sound of speech is made to match up to lip movements.

Take The filming of a particular shot.

Take-up spool The spool on which the tape is collected after it has passed through the VCR.

Telecine transfer A professional process by which images and sound can be moved from film to video, or from video to film.

Tracking shot A shot during which the camera is moved along during filming.

Zoom-in When the space between lenses in a camera is changed so that part of the image seems to come closer.

Index

Acknowledgements

Front cover background, Courtesy of Lucasfilm Ltd (LFL) © 1984 All rights reserved, Back cover, ITN ©, Endpapers, Ralph Nelson/Lucasfilm Ltd, 8 Martin Carter, Picture Post Films/R.N.L.I. 9 Jim Adams, 10 T.S.B. 14–15 BBC Hulton, 16–17 BBC Hulton, 18–19 National Film Archive, 20 Kobal Collection, 21 National Film Archive/MGMUA, 22 National Film Archive/20th Century Fox, 23 National Film Archive/MGMUA, 26/27 National Museum of Photography, Film & TV, 28 Granada Theatres, 29 Photri/Zefa, 31 Keith Hamshere/Lucasfilm Ltd., 35 E.M.I., 36–37 Tim Condren Stunt Co-ordinator, 39 Alex Salkind Presentation, 40–41 Courtesy of U.I.P., 44 Barry Fox, 45 Philips, 47 ITN, 50–51 Vestron Video © 1985 Tritec Music Ltd., 52 EMI, 54 Moving Pictures, 58 Popperfoto, 59 Colorsport, 60–61 Rex Features, 62–63 Philips, 65 Terry Staples, 67 Sheffield Film Co-op. 70 Avid Productions, 72/73 Richard Williams/United Artists TMC 1983, 74/75 National Film Archive, 76 Toshiba UK Ltd., 77 Channel Four, 78–79 Walt Disney, 82–83 Kobal Collection, 84–85 Lucasfilm Ltd., 86 Rank Videopro Systems Ltd., USIS, 87 Rank Videopro Systems Ltd., 88 Lucasfilm, 89 Panasonic.

Picture Research by Penny J. Warn.